A Lincolnshire Lad's Scrapbook
More Tales from Nocton Estate

First Published 2008

ISBN: 978 1 904686 16 3

A catalogue record for this book is available from the British Library

Published by
Japonica Press
Low Green Farm, Hutton, Driffield,
East Yorkshire, YO25 9PX
United Kingdom

Book layout by Banks Design

Acknowledgements

I would like to thank the friends who have helped me to produce this second book. The Redshaw family, whose late father was Mr Bill Redshaw, for the loan of many photographs; Mr Pete Ford for help with the captions and production of prints taken from photographs; Mrs Eddie Wakefield for photographs, and the many friends who have let me use their stories and poems. I would like to thank my friend Peter Lord for his computer knowledge, and the time and trouble he has taken to sort out my problems; the youngest computer wizard, my grandson Tom Pearson, who was only 11 years old when I wrote this book but already knew a lot more than I did about computers; my son Nigel and daughter Diane, for their support; John Tye for his visits; and of course all those who are included in the stories, for without them there would be no stories to tell.

There are three more people I must thank: my doctors, for the early diagnosis of Parkinson's disease - Doctor Parkin of the Branston Practice, who spotted the early signs and sent me to see Mr. Sharack, who straight away started my medication, which has kept me reasonably fit for the last seven years.

And finally my wife Pauline, for putting up with pictures and papers lying around the house for the last 3 years, and especially for all the hard work she has put in to help me produce this book.

Introduction

In May 2003 my book, A Lincolnshire Lad Looks Back, was published. It was mostly about my 45 years working on the Nocton Estate, between 1952 and 1997. Some of those who bought the book requested that, if I wrote a sequel, I could dwell more on the location of all the farmsteads and the social and sporting side of my life. I'll see what I can do! Firstly, though, for those who didn't buy my first book (which, incidentally, is still available from Japonica Press) I have compiled a short summary of my family history.

My father was a Wagoner at Todds Farm, Nocton Fen. He started work on the Nocton Estate at the age of 18 - the Estate was at that time owned by Mr J H Dennis. He married my mother, Nellie Crawford, and settled down at Todd's farm. Their first child was named Nellie, after my mother, then my brother Brian was born in 1935, and I was born in 1937. Later my mother had two more children, my brother Dennis and my sister Mavis.

Mr Dennis had bought Nocton Estate in 1919. He had seen how much a light

The author about to enjoy a meal some years previous

From Gautby in Lincolnshire a friend of mine by the name of Wink Carlton, who is getting well known in our part of the county for his old way of using the old English dialect, he has done quite a lot for charity

railway had been used in Europe during the Great War, so his Estate Manager of the time, Major Webber, bought second hand rolling stock, which had been used in Arras, France, and laid around 36 miles of narrow gauge track around the estate. Almost all of the farms were linked to the railway system; it was used to move produce from the water to the farms, and feed for the horses, pigs and beasts. At this time there were around 290 people employed on the estate. There were 220 heavy horses; a thousand cattle; three thousands pigs; two thousand sheep and a poultry unit.

The railway remained in use until it was replaced by rubber-tyred tractors during the 1950s and 60s.

In 1936 the estate was sold to Frank Smith, founder of Smith's Crisps, for the

New buildings with rail track prominent in the foreground

Driver Roy Sewell with one of the old railway locos

production of potatoes for his new enterprise. (Frank was to become a millionaire from a pinch of salt!) He was the son of a greengrocer, one of a family of 14 children. He began his working life as an errand boy fetching veg for his father's shop from Covent Garden – he would be there at 3 o'clock each morning, at only ten years old!

His ambition was to follow his father into the greengrocery business. He achieved this ambition, but he was restless, and in 1918 he threw up his job, and took a job with R Carter's Provisions in Smithfield, a company which had just started making crisps from sliced potatoes. He talked his way into the job of managing this department, then in 1920 he decided to have a go on his own.

He rented two garages in Cricklewood, and employed 12 people. They worked until one o'clock in the morning every day but Sunday, slicing potatoes. Frank would go out on his bike visiting pubs and clubs, selling his potato chips. People used to shout, 'I've got my chips, where is the fish?' Soon he hit upon the idea of introducing a pinch of salt twisted in a piece of blue paper. The salt made people thirsty, so the publicans loved him because they sold more beer.

The hall and grounds were sold in 1940 to the Ministry of Defence to build a hospital, after which the hall was sold to a businessman. In 1975 the estate was bought by the Guardian Royal Insurance group, for 3.5 million pounds, and a new farming company was born – British Field Products. It changed hands again in 1991 for 28 million pounds, and in 1995 was sold to the present owner, a Mr Clark.

The imposing residence of Nocton Hall

Typical cottage along the beckside at Dunston on the Nocton estate. This property today would command a high price

Frank Smith enjoys a rare moment of relaxation

Cottages at Nocton, showing old style architecture, March 1950

Farm buildings, yards and houses: A walk through the fen

We start our tour of the fen at the most easterly part of the Branston Fen. As you turn into the fen road off the Bardney Causeway, there used to be a small cottage occupied by a Mrs Dickinson, and for as long as I can remember the bridge at that point has been known as 'Dickinsons Bridge'.

Coming along the bottom of the fen, over the big drain on your left was a privately owned farm belonging to a Mr Peet. He mainly farmed pigs. When he retired his farm was bought by British Sugar and farmed by the Nocton Estate. The 90-odd acres over the river where the factory stands was part of the estate until the mid 1920s. All Nocton sugar beet, in the early days of the factory, was brought by loco to the iron pier-like structure you can still see spanning the river.

The beet was emptied into a holding pit on the west end of the pier. A grab travelled backwards and forwards across the river, taking one ton per trip and dropping it into a railway truck on the other side – it was then shunted into the factory flume area, where it was emptied by hand into the flume.

On Mr Peet's riverbank farm there was a footpath starting near Bardney Bridge

Bardney Beet Factory. Emptying loco railway trucks. In the background you can see the grab

Bardney Beet Factory

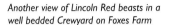

Lincoln Red beasts in an open Crewyard on Foxes farm

Another view of Lincoln Red beasts in a well bedded Crewyard on Foxes Farm

which went right across to Foxes road end. Some of the workers from Bardney used this path regularly to get to work. One chap noticed a chicken had made a nest under the straw stack near the footpath, and so he used to call each night on his way home and get himself a nice fresh egg for his tea. He did this for several weeks, but one day he went to put his hand under the chicken as usual when it ruffled its feathers and started clucking – it had turned broody. But not to be disappointed he picked up the chicken and pulled its neck, saying:

"You ode Bugger you, you're not gooin' ta dress me over!" - And he took it

home for Sunday dinner.

Getting back to our journey, coming along that bottom road the first farm road on your right led to Clarks Farm (we are in Potterhanworth Fen). At Clarks Farm there was a large farmhouse, and the farm buildings were two open hovels and a couple of barns, which are still there today. Until the 60's there was a stable and crew yard for eight horses, and then another crew yard for about fifty steers to winter.

There was also for many years a bale-walled, thatched roofed crew yard just over the dyke: it was built out of straw, roadside cuttings, and timber, all of which came from the Estate's wood mill.

Old and more modern pig stys. Ted Key seen mucking out into light railway wagon

Splendid row of cottages on the estate. Ten Row, Wellhead Lane, Nocton

In my early years the Cox family lived in the farmhouse. Arthur Cox was the waggoner. I remember an amusing tale of one harvest time, when a threshing gang sat down for tea. Bernard Andrews collected 2d from each man who wanted a can of tea from the house, and counted his money before he went to order the tea. He then announced:

"It looks as though all of you want a drink, there is eleven of us here without COX!"

(The harvest gang were Ralph Bainbridge, Tom Knowles, Harry Sherburn, Sid Goodyear, Harry Goodyear, Frank Smith, Arthur Cox, Ted Cooke, Son Cooke, Tom Overton, Albert Woodhead and Bernard Andrews).

The next people to live there were called Ablewhite, and as a school lad I was friendly with one of their lads, Pete, and spent quite a lot of time at the farm. I remember we went to Lincoln and bought a second hand wind up record player. We hadn't any records, though, until we saved up and biked to Spowges on the Cornhill in Lincoln and bought a '78' of Guy Mitchell's "Sipping Soda". That was the only record we had for weeks – didn't it get some playing!

Continuing our journey along the bottom road, the next farm road on our right led to Fox's Farm (we are still in Potterhanworth Fen). The road end is quite wide – it was widened to make a siding for the railway, as the beet was loaded onto lorries from the sidings and taken round to BSC. Later, as the farm roads were stoned and the lorries could get right up to the farms, it was time to say goodbye to the railway.

Bardney Causeway Cottages, which are now privately owned, were a pair of houses built for two stockmen in the 60's.

Fox's Farm was one of the main yards and housed the section foreman in charge of section C - the area of land was around 800 to 900 acres.

I described the farmhouse in my first book. It was the foreman's house, and my father was foreman from 1947 until he retired. I lived there from 1947 until I got married in 1960. The farmyard was a big area – the largest farmyard in the fens. There was a stable for about twelve horses and a crew yard for the horses to sleep in, also a block of four crew yards which held about twenty-five Hereford beasts each, during winter months. There was a large chaff house and a pig sty, a nice covered area for the horses, two large barns, one for fertilizer and one split in half, half made into a paddy house for the teams of Irish labourers who slept there during the harvest period, and the other half

Mechanics Ern Turner and Fred Tye attend to the John Deere in Ray's yard, Nocton. These buildings are now two desirable bungalows

The Shorthorn dairy herd in 1950. In the background we see a bale stack, a loose hay rick and a mix of traditional and more modern farm buildings

(which was locked up) was were Ben West the Garthman kept the food for his steers. Then finally two open cart hovels and a large pig crew at the rear.

When the farmyard was full of corn stacks, you could take a torch and an air rifle, and our dog Rex, and on a dark night in winter you could kill around thirty rats.

About 300 yards away from the main yard was a 120-ton capacity glasshouse, which was used for storing seed potatoes in the winter and for a crop of tomatoes during the summer.

Back to the bottom fen road and travelling south we come to another farm road on the right, this is the Glebe road. The large drain that runs alongside is the boundary between Potterhanworth Fen and Nocton Fen.

About half a mile down this road there used to be a straw crew yard, capable of housing about fifty steers during the winter. Then after another half a mile was Bottom Glebe Farm.

This farm had a barn and stable for four horses and crew yard, and a second crew yard for around fifty steers, or in some winters it held pigs.

I remember calling at the farmhouse to buy a tame rabbit once; the occupier took me upstairs to pick one and one bedroom was full of rabbits.

When these tenants left I helped them to carry their furniture out. When we moved it we could see that they had decorated the walls around the drawers, wardrobes and the rest of the furniture without moving it - you could have put it all back exactly where it had been before!

A further three quarters of a mile along this road there was another farmhouse and yard; this was Middle Glebe. There was a large barn, a crew yard for steers or pigs and a stable and crew yard for four horses. The barn is still standing; it is the home of the barn owls.

When I was thirteen years old I used to walk across the fields from Fox's to Middle

Bridge Farm Nocton Fen

Glebe some Saturday mornings to read the weekly mail to one of the regular Irishman who was living in the house. He used to pay me to do this - he couldn't read a word.

Back to the tarmac road, and after about another half mile a farm road goes off to our left, this leads to the Washway. On the right hand side of the road was a large piggery (it was in a stack in this yard that the stolen ham was found, you will read about this when you reach Mill Drain). Turning left into the Washway, just over the drain used to be a farmhouse, this was a nice little cottage for the pigman.

Continuing down this farm road towards the River Witham, at the point where now stands the new automatic pumping engine for the fens used to be a large red-bricked farmhouse and a small barn with a crew yard for over wintering bullocks.

Returning to the tarmac road, we come to Bridge Farm Corner. At this point there is a left turn over into the Washway - this was the road that in olden days took you down to the Wharf and the river. If you take this road over the drain and look southwards you will see in the distance, near the Nocton Delph, the old house used by the man who operated the pumping

engine still stands. When I was a lad there was a steam pump here that was fuelled by coal; it had a very tall chimney. If you have read my first book you may remember the story about a German fighter firing bullets at this chimney.

I think it would be in the late 40's when the steam engine was taken out and a Ruston Oil Engine was installed; it was used until the early 70's when it was replaced by an electric powered pump, which was then sited on the Witham instead of the Delph. The Ruston was taken out - we were told it was sold to the Philippines.

At this railway junction the householder had her water tank, and when I was a lad, we would sometimes bring a few small fish and drop them in this tank on the way home!

Back on our journey, from the tarmac road we now turn westward in the direction of the Wasps Nest. A few hundred yards along we can see Bridge Farm, this was a large red house and was the house for the B Section foreman. It had a large glasshouse and a stable for eight horses, a large barn, a converted barn made into living accommodation for eight to ten Irishmen, a crew yard and two open cart Hovels.

When I was a young lad the Flintham family lived here, and one of the daughters was called Phyllis. When she saw me coming she used to start singing:

"Lenny you're a funny'n, you have a face like a pickled onion, a nose like a squashed tomato and legs like match sticks".

When we kids got to be thirteen years old we could apply for a blue card in the late summer which, if you were successful, meant you could take three weeks off school in September and help the local farmers pick their potatoes. I remember one year we were a gang of twelve lads and lasses and we were picking potatoes in the field just past Bridge Farm. For those of you who are not familiar with picking potatoes, the foreman would come into the field and measure the length of the rows and then divide it by the number of pickers – in our case twelve. So say the field measured 120 yards long, he would measure 10 yards and put in a stick as a marker. He would then do this right across the field. The length between each stick we called wretches. The spinner would go down one side and come back down the other, when you had picked your 10 yards down one side level with your stick, you then walked across and picked your 10 yards down the other side.

One of the young lads lived in the fen with his Grandad, who used to come and help his grandson pick his wretch. Another lad, Nipper, noticed that when the Grandad stooped down to pick up some potatoes, he had a hole in his trousers which let his testicles hang out. This just suited Nipper, being a bit of a lad: he shouted to the young girl Elsie picking on the next wretch:

"Look at them two beauties – go and pick them, they look like potatoes!" Poor old Elsie turned all colours and didn't know what to do.

Back on the tarmac road, after about half a mile there is a farm road that turns off to the left. Down this road was Todds Farm, and the site of old buildings and two cottages that are no longer there. I was born in one of those cottages, in 1937. When I was a lad there was a stable where my father had four horses. There were two crew yards, one for the horses and one for the pigs. Also there were a couple of tractor sheds and an open hovel.

Three year old fat stock., Lincoln reds. Heathlands farm (Pawson's)

It's rather funny how you remember simple things: I remember one morning coming downstairs and going into the washhouse, which was a room big enough to have a sink and an old copper with a coal fire grate under it. I had quarry tiles about six inches square laid on the soil floor. I don't know how much a tile weighed, but a toadstool and grown in the night and lifted a floor tile, in fact it had flipped it over. That's the power of nature!

I have many happy memories of this farmyard. I remember learning to ride a bike, and getting on the bike one morning after being told off by my dad. I was in a bit of a rage so I was giving the bike some rough handling, and I went head over heels into a ditch full of stinging nettles. That settled it; I was so mad I jumped on the bike and away I went.

I remember the chickens making a hell of a noise one morning, and out came my mum from the house carrying a big clothes prop, to find a large snake after them. My mum soon clobbered it!

I also remember seeing the Southery men all coming to work on their bikes. Some of the men brought their food in a bag on their backs, but one or two had a small cane woven hamper on their carriers. One of these men was Herbert Johnson, and when I was about five years old I asked him:

"What have you got in that basket, Mister?" He laughed, and said:

"I've been pig killing, and I have got all the holes from a pig: his ear holes, his nose...." As he rode out of earshot he was still muttering something!

I remember when we were due to kill a pig in about a fortnight's time – it was one of the biggest we had ever had: over 30 stone. Dad got up one morning and said:

"I think it's got the purples." And so it had, and was soon dead, so Dad had to bike to Bardney, to the man who runs a pig club – like insurance – and he was able to get quite a lot of its money's worth paid back for us to buy a replacement.

If we travel through this yard towards the east we come to Washway Farm, where there was a fine big farmhouse, and the buildings were a four-horse stable and crew yard, two tractor houses, and a large open hovel. On one occasion the stockmen were just putting their horse away when an old lady came out of the house trying to keep the dog quiet. The beast had all gone out to grass that morning. She shouted to the dog:

"Moo cows all gone, Piggy Wiggy".

Another little story: The young chap who lived here when I was a lad was Arty Sewell. He went out one day and bought himself a real top of the breed ferret – it was a lovely white colour. On the Sunday morning he came across and said:

"Bring old Rover, and I'll take the ferret – I know where there's a few rabbits". So off we went – we put nets over all the holes but two – one was for the ferret to use, and old Rover guarded the other. But what a disaster: The first thing that bolted was the ferret, right under Rover's nose. One grab and a couple of shakes, and that was the end of that!

We now turn around and head back to Todds Farm. Just through the yards used to be a blacksmith's shop where they used to come and shoe the horses. It was at this point where I stood when the German fighter came past shooting at the pump chimney, as I described in my first book.

We make our way back to the tarmac road, turn left and head in the Wasp Nest direction.

After a short distance you come to another farm road, this time on your right. This leads to Hare Farm. This farmstead is about central to all of the fen part of Nocton Fen. Today you see about the only useful shed left in the fen. There used to be a nice sized house, a stable for eight horses, a crew yard, a small barn and an open cart hove. The thing that I remember about this farm is that Mrs Rollings, who lived in the house during the war, took in two small boys as part of the refugee arrangements. They were Gordon Leek and his brother Norman.

Back to the tarmac road, and turn towards the Wasp Nest again. Shortly you came to another farm road on your left: this was Mill Drain Farm. As you turned

Hare Farm, Nocton Fen

The Tomlinson brothers lifting a laid patch by hand on Middle Farm

Threshing corn at Lark Farm

left into the farm road, on the right side stood two really nice red brick houses – us kids once called there on Guy Fawkes night and we were given 2d – we had walked at least two miles!

Here's another story about a fine old Lincolnshire character, who happened to be short tongued. One harvest time, it was maybe 1953, there was a harvest gang leading corn and threshing at the extreme east of Fox's, say the farm road end. The Irishmen in the gangs would be in the fields picking up the sheaves from the stooks and loading them on the carts. With each cart you had to have someone to lead the horses, so one would be the waggoner (whose horses you were using) and the other during the summer holidays would be one of the older boys – that's where I came in. Now on some occasions the waggoner would take over the pitchfork from one of the three Irishmen in the field and he would help to load the cart while the Irishman had a rest by just leading the horse on from stook to stook. One day when the old

fellow had had lunch with the Irishmen he came to me and told me that because I was a small boy and couldn't do some of their work in the fields, the Irishmen had said 'that old boy is a dead ross'. Since that time and until he retired, every time I met the old chap he would say:

"You're a dead ross, boy!"

Carrying on down to the farmyard, there was a farmhouse; a large glasshouse; a stable for eight horses; two covered-in crew yards and an open cart hovel. At this farm during my childhood days Jack Franklin had killed a pig and I was cut up and laid curing in the pantry, covered in salt. One morning after breakfast h noticed one ham had gone. A few days later his lodger was arrested for theft: he had owned up and taken the police to the piggery, where they found the ham hidden in the straw stack.

Returning to the tarmac road, we turn left towards the Wasp Nest, and after another 300 yards we come to a farm road on the right which leads to Lark Farm.

Lark Farm was where the main blacksmith's shop was for the fen horses. There was a farmhouse; a stable for four horses; a large, partly covered (with corrugated iron) crew yard for about 100 steers; a barn and open cart hovel. It was at this farm where the last carthorse was used in the fen – it was used for a garth horse.

It was close to this farm that a Defiant crashed during the war.

I shall always remember a lad called Geoffrey, who seemed to be always on laxatives. He lived with his grandparents at Lark Farm. He sat near me in the second class at Nocton School, and on one particular morning the unfortunate happened, and Miss Nichols, the second class teacher at the time, soon smelt the problem…

"Geoffrey, go outside and get cleaned up. And Leonard, being as you know him well and he sits near you, go outside and help him, would you?" I didn't see much to laugh about but when I got up to go out the whole class was laughing.

Anyway, things weren't quite as bad as I thought they would be: Geoffrey was wearing Wellington boots, so most of the mess was in his boots – he soon had them off and under the tap, and then I fetched some old newspapers for him to clean the inside of his trousers.

Another classroom story: I sat near a pal we called Nipper, and we were sat together in the infant class, and one day I noticed he had got his willy out and was playing with it under the desk. I wasn't the one to notice – Miss Turner, our teacher, saw him, and told him not to be so naughty and put it away, which he did immediately. He told me that one of the big lads told him that the more you play with it the bigger it gets – I wouldn't mind finding out if the advice from the big lad had turned out to be right or not!

Modern grain store, chitting house, old factory and a straw bale shelter for the Essex pigs, show the diversity of buildings on this Fenland estate

Once again back to the tarmac road, and turning right towards Wasp Nest, after another half mile we head off to the left, to Decoy Farm. This farm was so named because many years ago, when land around this area was boggy and part flooded, gamekeepers used to put out decoy ducks for a few days before a duck shoot would take place.

The farmhouse was a large one and built with red brick. This is the farm where George Wakefield started work (he was mentioned in my first book). There was a stable for eight horses, and two crew yards – one for the horses, and one for pigs; a large barn, which was partly made into a place for Irish labourers to lodge, and two open hovels.

About 500 yards further along the tarmac road there was a nice red brick bungalow on our left, then a right turn to Partridge Farm: This is the farm where my father started as a boy of 18, as second chap in a stable with eight horses.

The head waggoner was a chap called George Reeve, who eventually set himself up with a lorry, and after a while he soon had a fleet.

Apart from the eight-horse stable there was a barn, which was partly made into an Irish abode, and two crew yards, one for horses and one for pigs or bullocks. In my first book I wrote about the irrigation system - this is the point where the water had to be lifted over a six foot dam to enable it to get up to the Wasp Nest.

The last tenant in the house used to burn anything he could – he used to carry long pieces of wood into the house, and never used to saw it into logs: he would stand a chair a few feet away from the fire and with one end almost up the chimney, as the fire burned the end off he would just push the wood further into the fire from the other end. When he moved out of the house we found many farm tools under the stairs – he had burned all the shafts or handles off them. He was a man who was a bit on the tight side: he would wear any size of footwear from a size eight to eleven. I once saw him with a green Wellington on one foot and a black one on the other.

Heading back to the tarmac road, and continuing towards Wasp Nest, there was a farmhouse and buildings on the right, which have now been demolished. This was Middlefield Farm. We used to come here carol singing. One Christmas Eve, after a few drinks at the social club at Wasps Nest, we decided to go out and sing a few carols. We first made a trip around the Wasp Nest houses, then we thought that we might just go and see Daisy at Middlefield Farm. So off we went, and we sang a few carols, then I noticed she had left her washing out on the garden line…and there was a row of cabbages, just nicely hearted…so I got my pocket knife out and cut a cabbage for each pair of bloomers on the line, we put a cabbage in each and away we went.

The farmyard had an open cart hovel; a barn and a stable for four horses.

We are now close to Wasp Nest itself, but before we get to this small hamlet, I want to mention two houses down Potterhanworth Fen, next to Battles Farm. The spot is marked by a well where we fetched our drinking water from when we lived at Fox's Farm. I remember the droves of rats at night. Alan, who lived at the farm as a lad, used to get some long, thin willow branches, and by using copper wire he would make a snare. He would bend it down so the snare was on the rat run, and hook it in that position. As the rat ran along it would go head first into the snare and knock it off its catch. Up into the air would go the rat, the snare pulling its neck out as it went skywards. I have been down with him in the morning and seen the rats hanging in the snares.

WASP NEST

As we come towards the Wasp Nest from the fens, on your left you come to two open hovels. These used to be two crew yards holding about 50 beast through the winter. They are now used as implement sheds, except for one end which has been made into a chemical store, and also sitting on an old Scott pea viner chassis is a large water tank fitted with a ball cock system to

Corn drier and storage bins. Furnace house in the foreground

Noton Fen. Wasp Nest. One of the new Baker bilt Crewyards

the water main. If we now go to the tarmac road, but go straight across, passing the small pump house and reservoir on your left, at this point the water is pumped into an underground main and transferred to the heath system. After travelling down this road you eventually come to a sharp corner. This is Willow Junction. It was at this point that there used to be another straw crewyard.

Turning back and to the right, the main buildings are now straight in front. The first houses are on the right. One was for a waggoner, and the other for the head gamekeeper – they are still there today; I believe the gamekeeper has bought them.

Next where the large potato store now stands was a stable and crewyards for at least eight horses. We now move on to the red house on the right: this used to be the Foreman's house when there were sections, but lately it has been the home of the head gamekeeper. Next, right on the corner, is a large corrugated zinc hovel. Over the Carr Dyke there is a row of four houses – they used to be for the Nocton workers. (They are still there, but may not be four now).

Further along there are some houses, which are now private, but when they were built they were agricultural council houses. On the hill behind these used to stand the Was Nest Village Hall and Social Club – erected in 1947 and closed in 1959.

Moving round the corner on your right was another farmhouse occupied by a waggoner, and there was also a stable, barn and crew yard, and then finally there stood a large glasshouse.

That completes the fen farms and houses. That's thirty houses plus the council houses that were all occupied by the estate workers in my early days in the fen. With the lack of electricity and water supply, and a government move to charge rates for empty houses, as they became empty they were pulled down.

You can see now how big a community there was around Wasp Nest. The houses and farms I have mentioned are just a small number of the houses owned by the estate – there were some in Dunston Fen and what we call the middles, the heath farms, and also the two villages of Nocton and Dunston.

29th December 1956 - Goodbye Mr Crisp

The man who built his fortune with a pinch of salt in a little blue bag died yesterday, 28th December. He was Mr Frank Smith, a grocer's boy. He was the 7th son of a 7th son, and he made all the other Smiths sit up and stare, when he made his fortune, starting with nothing and with no help. With his crisps he changed the eating habits of half the world.

He was from a family of 14. His first dealings with potatoes was when, at 3 o'clock each morning, he collected potatoes from Covent Garden for his father's grocers shop. He was ten years old then, and his ambition was to follow in his father's footsteps. He achieved his ambition at the age of 21. He was restless in his father's business, and in 1913 he chucked his

Mrs Frank Smith and Mr and Mrs Cyril Scott desire to express their deep appreciation of your sympathy with them in their recent bereavement.

January, 1957.

NOCTON FARMS LTD.

The S.P.C.

SMITH'S

Quarterly Magazine

HOUSE JOURNAL OF SMITHS POTATO CRISPS LIMITED
OCTOBER, 1954
VOL. XXIV. No. 93.

A 1954 front cover of the house journal of Smith's Potato Crisps Limited.

manager's job and joined R Carter, a grocery provision firm. They had just started a new line which they called potato crisps. Young Smith talked his was into taking charge of this new department. Then in 1920 he decided to branch out on his own. He rented two garages in Cricklewood, and set on a staff of 12 to cut up the potatoes. They all worked until one o'clock in the morning, six days a week.

Everyone laughed at him as he peddled his crisps around the pubs – some drinkers shouted 'Where's the fish?' But Smith was persistent and it was here that he thought up his gimmick of adding a little blue bag of salt. The salt made the drinkers thirsty so the publicans adored him, and they sold and advertised his crisps as hard as they could.

Seen at the 1962 Commercial Motor Show, this Albion 4 ton Chieftain was exhibited on the Normand stand displaying the Smith's livery

I am a record potato – my variety is grown just for crisps

And I come from a place called the Nocton Estate, which is owned by Smiths Potato Crisps

It is April in the year of 1949. I had been in a crate with hundreds of other potatoes, in a large greenhouse. Through the winter months I was kept at around 40 degrees Fahrenheit. An iron brazier fire was lit to keep me warm and free from frost. In early March the greenhouse temperature was allowed to rise by about 10 degrees. This made me open my eyes and I started to grow small shoots.

Now I am loaded onto a trailer or cart and taken out into a field where there are men and horses working, making long, straight ridges right across the field. I am picked out of the crate and laid in the bottom of a ridge, with another potato about 10 inches on either side of me. After a while some horses come towards me and almost tread on me, but then I realise I am in the dark.

After about six weeks I peep through the soil and it is daylight. My shoots keep growing, and within a few weeks I am producing baby potatoes. As time passes those baby potatoes grow bigger and bigger, until they are about as big as me.

The Smith's Potato Crisps stand at the Earls Court Evening News Flower Show, August 1952

Any produce moved on the farm was recorded

SMITHS POTATO ESTATES LTD.				No 5017			

From FIELD No. *W N I* Date *24th Sept* 1949

DELIVERED To *RAILHEAD*

Per TRUCK No. *6*

LORRY No.

DESCRIPTION	SACKS No.	STS.	KIND	VARIETY	T.	C.	Q.
POTATOES	60	8	B/W	RECORD	3	0	0
WHEAT							
BARLEY							
OATS							
PEAS							
BEET							
BEANS							
	60	8	B/W		3	0	0

Signed (SENDER) *L Woodhead*

Signed (RECEIVER) *D Turner*

SMITHS POTATO ESTATES LTD.				No 5017			

From FIELD No. *W N I* Date *24th Sept* 1949

DELIVERED To *RAILHEAD*

Per TRUCK No. *6*

LORRY No.

FOR OFFICE USE
By
To
Trk. No.
Ref. No.

DESCRIPTION	SACKS No.	STS.	KIND	VARIETY	T.	C.	Q.
POTATOES	60	8	B/W	RECORD	3	0	0
WHEAT							
BARLEY							
OATS							
PEAS							
BEET							
BEANS							
	60	8	B/W		3	0	0

Signed (SENDER) *L Woodhead*

Signed (RECEIVER) *D Turner*

It doesn't seem long before a tractor and a funny machine called a potato spinner threw me and all the other potatoes out on the top of the ground. Then I am picked up by a young lady and put into a wooden cane hamper, until along comes another person and empties all of us into a cart, which takes us to the end of the field. Then the cart tips up and we all tumble out onto the ground. A man scoops us up with a shovel-like tool and lifts us up onto a round thing called a riddle. So here I am being shaken backwards and forwards in the riddle until all the loose soil and shoots are shaken off me, and I am a lovely bright, clean potato.

I am tossed into a hessian sack and more potatoes are put on top of me, and eventually the sack is closed and tied up. I am loaded onto a small truck, and the man in charge gets out a ticket book and fills in a ticket with the date and field, what the crop was and the variety, and how much was loaded on the truck. One part of the ticket is put into a small tin box on the front of the truck, and the other part is kept by the man in charge, then a train comes along, fastens onto the truck and takes us to Nocton & Dunston Station, where we are carried off and loaded onto the big British Rail train, which takes us to a Smiths Potato Crisp factory.

A stand at a trade show, showing not just potatoes, but a diverse variety of crops. The board at the front says 'Produce from our own farms"

Bog Oaks

Way back in history, trees such as oak, fir, yew, alder and willow grew in our fens, but no ash, and very few elms. There was never a forest, just small areas of trees. The oaks grew more on the boulder clay, which was formed in the Great Ice Age, and were later uprooted by the flood gravels. In this stratum and in the peat areas grew the fir, yew, alder and willow.

Over hundreds of years these trees died and rotted off in the peat, or were knocked down by the strong storms and tides. There are still hundreds of them today, just below ploughing level. At Nocton, over my 50 years, lots have been dug out, especially down by the Witham - some with large girths and up to 90 feet long.

If you stand at a high point such as Ely Cathedral and look across the thousands of acres which are now farmed, think back to Roman times and imagine what a tremendous difference there must be in the landscape.

Mr J Ireson, one time manager of Smith's Potato estate, once said:

"Agriculture, which is the first calling of mankind, is the most honest, the most useful and consequently the noblest profession that man can exercise."

Track-Marshall 55 with deep digger plough. A plough of this type would often unearth bog oaks

On that horrible wet day....

If we were rained off our job and we had to take cover, there were several things we used to do. We were mostly on piece-work, so no work, no money. Sometimes, depending on the time of year, the fore-man would have some jobs you could do undercover, for which you would be paid by the hour, but other times when a group got together someone would suggest we 'stick the knife up'.

That meant someone getting their pocket knife out and sticking it in the ground, then a mark would be drawn about 8 to 10 feet away from it, and out would come the pennies. The idea of the game was that everyone threw a penny to the knife and the one whose penny fell nearest the knife would pick up all the coins, place them on the back of his outspread hand and toss them in the air. The ones that dropped down showing heads were his to keep and the remainder, which of course would be tails, were tossed by the second nearest and so on until all the coins had been won.

Some of the young men used to arm-wrestle, and some of the really tough ones would see how far they could carry some-thing heavy, maybe a sack of potatoes or fertiliser – one hundredweight bag under each arm, and maybe even a third on the shoulders.

Another strong man thing was to get a 4 stone iron weight off a weighing machine and see who could throw it up the highest, maybe over a beam in the wagon hovel.

On certain wet days it would be time for a couple of men to get out their clip-pers and give most of the gang a haircut.

You made your own fun to pass away the time – sometimes you were like kids, playing tricks on your mates. I remember when we used to go to Bardney Sugar Beet factory to fetch sludge lime. Some of the lorry drivers used to go early to get that extra load, but when the majority of the other hauliers came in the early birds were often asleep at the front of the queue, wait-ing for the loader driver to come to work. A few of us used to get some rope and tie it round the back of the cab and to the door handles, so when they woke up they found they were left behind, and the other driv-ers had been loaded first.

Tha Knaws

Allan Carter, a real Yorkshire man, came to the Estate as a lorry driver in the late 50's. During his time here he became secretary to the Estate football club, and was well known for his Yorkshire accent. The following poem about him was published in the SPC quarterly magazine.

Allan Carter on his wedding day

A Yorkshire man, and rather small.
A face that's...well...not pretty
A voice that carries far and wide
And this, we know, his ditty:
                        THA KNAWS.

From John O'Groats back to Lands End
He knows the corners well
But sure as his name is what it is
He'll drive us all to...Well,
                        THA KNAWS.

His runner beans are quite well known
His onions take some beating
His stories about BOC
Are hardly worth repeating
                        THA KNAWS.

His favourite run was Potter Fen
Down the Bardney Causeway
Up to the top of Fox's Road
And is he really Sausey?
                        THA KNAWS.

He's driven everything that goes
On wheels of course I mean
A Dennis, Mase or was it Pase
But does he keep them clean?
                        THA KNAWS.

His Tumbler polish takes the cake
It sparkles in the sun
He cleans the windows sometimes too
Which causes quite some fun
        THA KNAWS.

At spanner sizes he's red hot
Three eight or five sixteen
But razor blades seem very scarce
If you see what I mean
        THA KNAWS.

At tipping beet into the flumes
Sometimes he makes a slip
And tips it in a heap on top
Which makes him bite his lip
        THA KNAWS.

As football sec. he is superb
His knowledge is uncanny
His thirst for points leads him astray
In fact it drives him scranny
        THA KNAWS.

And when he's speeding down the road
The roadmen give him space
They drop their tools, jump off the road
And ask for saving grace
        THA KNAWS.

'I nivver thote' is what he said
When tipping up the water
The ganger said 'Get out of sight'
The driver said we oughter
        THA KNAWS.

Among his pals are well big knobs
Lord Mayor and Town Clerk
Seems Magistrates are more the line
But let us keep that dark...
        WE KNAWS.

The writer, he is rather shy
His job is just the same
He writes is lines in his spare time
No need to sign his name...
        HE KNAWS.

An ode to the EEC

'Won't you join our Common Market?'
Said the Spider to the Fly
It really is a winner
And the cost is not too high.

I know DeGaulle said 'Non'
But he hadn't got a clue
We want you in, my friends,
And we have plans for you

You'll have to pay a little more
Than we do - just for now,
As Herr Kohl said, and I agree,
We need a new 'Milch Cow'.

It's just a continental term
Believe me, mon ami,
Like 'Vive La France'
'Mad Anglaise' or even 'EEC'

As to the rules, don't worry, friend,
There's really but a few,
You'll find that we ignore them
(But they do apply to you).

Give and share between us,
That's what it's all about
You do all the giving,
And we will share it out.

It's very British, is it not,
To help a friend in need
You've done it twice, in two World Wars
A fact we must concede.

So climb aboard the Market Train
Don't sit there on the side
Your Continental Cousins
Want to take you for a ride.

Bob Wydell

Sports at Nocton

Nocton Estate football club 1961-62

Back row: P. Roberts, L. Saunby, R. Redshaw, K. Redshaw, T. Fox, R. Parker, K. Johnson, B. Tye, C. Redshaw, M. Roberts, J. Roberts Front Row: A. Day, Muxslow, Trip, J. Mackey, B. Stephenson

NOCTON ESTATE F.C. - SEASON 1950-51
back l-r: D. Gash, F. Atkin, T. Asher, G. Chambers, R. Mason, K. Melton, T. Jackson, S. Fenwick, B. Watson, E. Parker
front l-r: T. Richardson, H. King, T. Melton, B. Johnson, A. Bee

Nocton FC - 1957
back l-r: P. Goodyear, W. Watson, J. Moody, A. Todd, B. Woodhead, D. Tye, G. Gash, E. Turner, S. Goodyear.
front l-r: J. Chambers, D. Moody, R. Redshaw, R. Blackband, F. Turner

Nocton Estates FC - 1936-37
five across back:- Harry Allgood, Jack Brampton, ?, Arthur Rashby, Percy Ward
middle l-r: ?, Bob Foster, Horace Wright, Syd Evans, Tommy Harding, Fred Doughty, Tommy Melton Snr, K Buckberry, Arthur Damsett, Alf Temple, George Rasen, Fred Elvin, ?(glasses), ?White shirt, ??, "Sailor Warman, Sam Leggett, ?
front l-r: Herbert Halstan, Walt Temple, Jim Burge, Fred Willeford, Bob Peak, Tommy Melton jnr.

NOCTON CRICKET CLUB - 1960
back l-r: T. Fox, A. Day, R. Lowin, K. Johnson, T. Turner, B. Chambers, C. Bryan
front l-r: F. Wilford, C. Pask, R. Parker, R. Redshaw

Lincoln League Division Two winners - 1955, Nocton Cricket Club proudly display their trophy. Back row left to right: Umpire, Ally Bee, Roy Redshaw, Mrs D. Asher (scorer), Norman Harvey, T. Hendry, Robert Pask. Front left to right: Dawn Turner, Fred Willford, Charlie Bryan, John Ireson (president and also estate General Manager), Chick Pask, Ray Lawin, Dick Creasey

School Sports Day

When Vinegar Joe came to Tupholme Hall

On the 16th June 1972 there was the biggest invasion that I had ever seen in our part of the world, when a weekend pop festival was held at historic Tupholme Hall. There were thousands of cars, motorbikes and walkers, with all sorts of tents, and the 700 acre estate was awash with people. As it happened, it rained, it rained and it rained, making it difficult to travel or to walk, but the show went on. It was estimated that there were 40,000 people there.

The wind blew the beer cans about, and anything else that was light enough to move. Old sheets that had been fixed up as tents were blown away, and some of the better tents too.

The groups were 'The Strawbs', 'Vinegar Joe' and 'Sha Na Na'. Some of the neighbours on the Tupholme estate had a few problems. The local paper told that Mrs Lucy Newton had to move into the back bedroom because of the noise. Mr Robert Armstrong had to chase someone out of his wheatfield, and said that once in a lifetime was enough. But Mrs Esther Quibell said it was nice to see people around. Overall it wasn't much of a problem, and it was estimated that the village of Bardney was richer by some £100,000 – the people with the brains made the money. It was planned to hold more festivals, but up to now we haven't had any more.

RMLIFE

B1202 BARDNEY

Pop Festival

AA

Mr. Robert Armstrong— "Once in a lifetime is enough."

Mrs. Esther Quibell—"It's nice to see some life around here."

Mr. George Massey — "Shall we have people hanging around waiting for the next one?"

Mrs. Lucy Newton—"We had to move into a back bedroom."

When Vinegar Joe came to Tupholme Hall

Dad's furniture bill

My Dad and Mum got married and went to live at Todds Farm in March 1932.

My Dad's furniture bill was:

Bedroom Suite   £10
Table   £2/2/-
4 x Leather Chairs @ 7/6d each £1/10/-
Armchair   £1/2/6
Ladies Cane Chair   £1/2/6
Oak Sideboard   £4/10/-
Mirror   5/11
Wringer   £2
Dolly Tub   5/11
Pegs 3/6
Clothes Basket   2/6
Fire Kerb   12/6
Clothes Horse   16/-
2 Bedsteads @ £1/16/- each   £3/12/-
2 Sprung Mattresses @ £1/15/- each £3/10/-
2 Wool Mattresses @ £1/15/- each £3/10/-
2 Feather Beds @ £1/1/- each   £2/2/-
Chamber Set 10/6
Clock   £2/10/-
Wash Tub   7/6
Two buckets @ 9d each   1/6
Coal hod   1/11
4 x chairs @ 7/6 each   £1/10/-
Tea set   15/-

Total: £55/10/2d

All bought from Neale Bros., High Street, Lincoln

A Lincolnshire agricultural railway

A GLIMPSE OF THE PAST: 1957

Tommy Asher operates one of the railway junctions in 1950. Note the variety of rolling stock

Travelling with British Rail on the Lincoln & Spalding line, when you passed through Nocton & Dunston station it was possible to see a small, narrow-gauge railway system. Small engines with trucks loaded with farm produce used a 1ft 11 _ in. gauge rail line, probably the only one in the country at that time using this gauge on around 33 miles of track running over almost all of the Smith's Potato Estate.

The system was expertly run by a Traffic Controller, using strict timetables to plan movement of all engines at all times. Almost every field and farmyard on the estate was linked. Hundreds of tons of potatoes, sugar beet, wheat and barley were moved daily from field to railhead.

The 8000-acre estate had been bought by Smith's Potato Crisps Limited in 1936,

The area stretched from the River Witham near Bardney to Waddington Airfield. The land was really bought for growing potatoes for delivery to the Smiths crisp factories, but because of the disease factors they could only grow potatoes on each field every three years, later to be stretched to seven. But this worked very well on the 8000 acres, and a good crop rotation could be used.

The previous owner, a Mr W Dennis, had bought the railway system from the War Department in 1921 – it had originally come from France. Only a short length of rails was laid at first, but owing to its success it was continued throughout the estate in 1926. Some of the track was laid on metal sleepers and some on wood. The main depot was near Nocton and Dunston mainline station. Here there was quite a large rail network of sidings; some were fitted alongside British rail, as quite a lot of produce was loaded onto the British rail network.

It was quite a scenic ride from the railhead to the bottom of the fens. You first travelled alongside the grotto, and soon afterwards you passed the hospital next to Nocton Hall on your left, then through some clumps of trees until you came to the top of Abbey Hill, from here on most days you could see right across the fens. On very clear days you could see the Lincolnshire Wolds, and looking to your left, the great Lincoln Cathedral standing magnificently on the hill.

When you first started to descend Abbey Hill, you were right above the lovely hamlet of Wasp Nest. The line then levelled out across the fens, crossing large drains and bridges, right to the River Witham.

One of the main haulage jobs for the rail system was to take sugar beet to Bardney. About 300 yards from the river a weighbridge was installed, and all the beet crop was hauled by rail and weighed at this point before being taken down to the river, where the trucks were emptied by hand into a pit, to be carried over the iron bridge by a grab one ton at a time. The iron bridge still spans the river today, as it has done since 1928.

The railway rolling stock consisted of 36 small trucks which were four wheeled, and we called them ration trucks as they would carry about half a ton each – this was just about right for the weekly rations for each farmyard's heavy horses. If the farmyard had other stock in its crew yards then a larger, 6 ton truck would be used for rations. There were 54 open bogie wagons,

five water tanks – some of these were used to collect the rainwater off the workshop buildings, and are still there today – and 12 box wagons, which had been used as ambulances during their time in France.

Two of the trucks were converted to fuel wagons to deliver tractor fuel weekly to the 40 tractors around the estate. One of the better ones was made into a passenger coach – this was for transporting the guns around the estate on shoot days.

There were 6 Simplex diesel locomotives, one having been stripped of some of its cladding to help ground clearance in the boggy areas.

When the locos first came to Nocton they had petrol engines, but in the 1930s they were fitted with diesel engines. They were all fitted with sanders to help them travel through the fens more easily: they could move very well with a 12 ton load.

For a short while a 0-4-0 Fowler steam tank engine weighing 13 tons was used, but it was too heavy for the track so it was confined to working the higher part of the estate. At one stage it was used as a shuttle service hauling from Wasp Nest, where it could pull more tonnage up Abbey Hill to the railhead. Later, other forms of transport replaced the whole system as the farm roads were stoned, lorries and then rubber tyred tractors and trailers could link up even better to fields and depot. And of course the poor old horse was replaced as well.

Eric Hardy and colleague loading potatoes at the railhead

An ode to the railhead

Our new General Manager Mr Ireson, his motto is just swell:
"If we set out to do a job, let's try and do it well".
Messrs Treavett, Brown and Carradice in the office work all day
Busy with Income Tax, accounts and rates of pay.
Supervising all repairs on a large estate like this
Is Mr Ingall's problem, there's not much he does not miss.

Our chief mechanic, Freddie – his second name is Tye –
At any job that needs repair, be sure he'll have a try
Assisted by young Ernie, who is picking up the trade
His experience in driving will help him make the grade.
Next on the list comes Heeming, assisted by son Fred
Who repairs the carts and wagons, and paints them all deep red.

There's Chris and Jack, good men they are, and any job can do
Strike while the iron's very hot, and horses they can shoe.
At implement repairs no better men we've got
Than Genial George I'Anson, he'll weld the blinking lot!
If it's nuts or bolts or anything you require from the store
Our friend Leeming's got from the ceiling to the floor.

Fred Tye in the well equipped mechanics shop

Ern Turner, Fred Tye and Maurice Hubbard, hard at work in the workshop

Jack Bond and 'Ally' Bee are seldom ever seen
They each do drive a lorry, so very smart and clean.
Then next comes our pal Edgar, who on the anvil strikes,
If the work is complicated, then that's the job he likes.
We must not forget the turner and fitter of some fame
Who takes an interest in his work, and Elvin is his name.

Then Jim the engine driver, Ruston's engines he does drive,
He puts the 'juice' into the lines and makes them all alive.
If there's any bricks want laying, or building to be done,
Just think of Ted and Harry who use concrete by the ton.
The twenty-five miles of railway, it always needs repair,
It wants two men as you can guess, so Matt and George are there.

And then the loco drivers: Dick, Hector, Jack and Ted,
Transporting potatoes, corn and rations from Fen to Railhead.
There's lots of bags and sacking that needs sorting for repairs
So if you can go into the stores, you'll find Jack Coleby there.
We must not forget our Dora, the only female on the staff –
At times she looks so serious, she really makes you laugh.

Then Maurice in the Mill, grinding corn up by the ton;
When his day's work is finished he's soon shooting pigeons with his gun.
Now Smith, the Mill assistant, his nickname it is 'Bud',
He keeps the machines running, at that he's very good.
Control of all the railway is in charge of our friend Reg,
He always know the records of the files up on the ledge.

But don't forget the guard boys who couple up each train,
They're out in all the weathers: hail, sun or driving rain.
And Philip and young Derek, apprentices they are,
They do all sorts of little jobs, their future don't lets mar
Now readers, this ode is finished, and it's very plain to see
We all work well together, and as happy as can be.

Then take coats off to the future, and hats off to the past:
A new era is dawning, lets strive to make it last.

I W Ingall, 1946

Goodbye Bonnie and friends

I am writing this poem in a very sad way
Thinking about farming and the change here today.
All the work we have done has been long days and tough
And the money we were paid was never enough.

When I left school I was ready and keen
To be a Waggoner like my Dad had been.
But I hadn't worked long, I had just made a start
When poor old Bonnie was changed for a Fergy and cart.

In the early 50s when I started work in the Fen
I didn't realise what was happening then.
Harry Ferguson, away in the USA
Had fitted hydraulics on tractors in grey.

The tractor he built could do everything, of course
Things didn't look good for poor Captain, my horse.
Bonnie and friends in the stable were soon loaded and gone
The tractors were doing the jobs they had done.

Instead of ridging two acres a day
They were now doing ten acres or more, they say.
And when loesing time comes the tractor just drives in the shed
But old Captain needs supper, and then putting to bed.

And at weekends old Captain still needs feeding every day
But no-one need look at Harry Fergy just stood in the bay.
The day will come soon - and I don't want Captain to hear -
When down the road comes a lorry, it's for Captain I fear.

I have dreaded this day, never thought it would come
When the Foreman came round, he said 'What have you done?
Open those doors, Captain's not going today,
I need him for gathering, the cows need some hay'.

And when the time comes, and Captain is beat
I'll take him to old Harold and I will pay for his keep.
Old Captain has worked with us for over ten years,
He deserves a good retirement, I'm sure there'll be tears.

Len Woodhead

Ian Spofforth unloads chitting trays off the horse drawn cart. Note the drop sides to form a wide platform

Fred Glossop harrowing with a fine team of horses

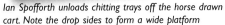

Loading the rulley with straw at Manor Yard, Nocton

Harvesting potatoes, horse and tractor power working side by side

Mr. Hemmings and his son Fred busy in the wheel-wrights shop

Bill Glossop, Jack Worrell, George Redshaw and Les Saunby drilling beans and covering with light harrows. Probably the last horses to be used on the estate

Livestock on the Estate

A prize winning Essex gilt

Pedigree Essex sows and gilts tuck in to a meal on Todd's Farm, Dunston

A lively looking pen of gilts, Webster's Yard, Dunston

Contentment! Hall's Yard, Dunston

The Dairy Shorthorn herd, Manor Farm, 1950. Few dairy herds remain in the County of Lincolnshire today

The dairy herd was dispersed in 1955, interestingly the catalogue gave a list of convenient hotels for potential buyers to stay including the White Hart, Lincoln (phone 26!)

NOCTON
LINCOLNSHIRE
7½ miles S.E. from Lincoln.

IMPORTANT DISPERSAL SALE OF THE ENTIRE

" LADYMEER " HERD

OF

ATTESTED

DAIRY SHORTHORNS
(Under the Shorthorn Society's Auction Rules)

THE PROPERTY OF MESSRS. SMITH'S POTATO ESTATES LTD., DAIRY FARM, NOCTON, LINCOLN (who are giving up Dairy Farming)

ON

Monday, 26th September, 1955

Sale (Under Cover) to commence at 1-30 p.m.

AUCTIONEERS:
JOHN H. WALTER & SONS
Lincoln

Pedigree Lincoln Red stock bull, three and a half year old "Benbridge"

A yard of Lincoln Red young stock. Note the thatched corn stack in the background.

The shoot

The Nocton Shoot has been well known for many years as one of the best in the country. Records of the shoot go back to the mid-30s and beyond.

Back in the 1800s Earl de Grey (later the Marquis of Ripon) was recorded to have shot 1000 pheasants with just one gun in one season.

The best bag ever recorded in one season was in 1935-6 when 4122 pheasants and 1904 partridges were shot.

The highest number of rabbits shot in one season was in 1936-7, the number was 4382. And the record for hares was in 1952-3, when 1244 were shot.

Years ago, there were a tremendous number of English partridges breeding wild across the Fens. They flew low and weaved about, making them harder to shoot. These attracted the better guns across the country, as it was more of a challenge. They have become fewer over the last 20 years, mainly because of slow disappearance of the insects and pale percycaries (willow weed). Now, with the barn owls and harriers coming back, they will be lucky to survive.

The marsh harrier nested in the Fen in 1994, for the first time in about 25 years. The pair reared four young, and have returned and nested every year. By the year 2003 there were around ten pairs nesting. Can you imagine the amount of rabbits, hares, rats, mice and young pheasants and partridges these birds of prey would need to collect to feed their broods?

Eustace Pask with Gamecart - 1947

Recently some of the smaller and more common birds of prey, such as the magpie and the jay, were often shot, because of the eggs they would steal from nests in the Spring. Nowadays, with all the owls and harriers, it is better to buy in pheasant and partridge eggs and hatch them off in incubators. They are kept safely penned up until they are half-grown, then release them into the wild in late June and July.

The main problem with this is that the English partridge doesn't breed very well in captivity, so the red legged French partridge is gradually replacing it.

So the gamekeeper's job is rearing and feeding birds, trapping vermin, controlling rats and mice, patrolling for poachers (and also a more recent menace, the hare coursers, with their greyhounds), and on some occasions pigeon control.

The guns seem well pleased with their bag

An in-depth discussion probably on which field to draw first

Break time for the beaters. The wooden crate of beer seems to be well received

Nocton and Dunston garden fetes

Garden fetes were held regularly to raise funds for the Estate football club, the cricket club, the Church and the old folks' club. The usual venue was in the Hall grounds, given permission of the Commanding Officer of the Norton RAF Hospital, who would usually be asked to open the fete. Sometimes they would be held in the Embassy grounds (the farm general manager's house), in which case they would be opened by the Estate manager or his wife. On other occasions they would be opened by a visiting dignitary, some I remember were Sir Sydney King, from the Agricultural Workers Union; Lord Neville, Lord Lieutenant of Lincolnshire, and the Lord Mayor of Lincoln, Alderman Flintham.

At a garden fete there would often be a game of skittles for a six-week-old pig, worth about £6 or £7. There would be nine skittles set up on a 4ft square board; you paid your 6d and were given three cheeses. You stood behind a marked line about ten yards away and threw the cheeses at the skittles. The highest score of the number you managed to knock down with your three cheeses was recorded, and the person who knocked the most down would get the pig.

Then there would be bowls, this was a simple sort of game: a board with five numbered holes in it was set up, you had six balls and you rolled each one to try and score as much as you could. At the end of the fete the one with the highest score would win a bottle of whiskey – now that was something, they were very rare and very expensive. (There was a separate prize for children!)

Another game involved a 3ft wide wooden trough about 15ft long. You rolled a ball down the trough, and it hit a piece of wood at the end, bounced up and landed in a numbered compartment in a box. You had six or maybe eight wooden balls, and the highest score won the prize.

'Roll a Penny' was a table marked out in small squares; you rolled your pennies down small chutes and if it landed in a square without touching a line you got it back, and an extra one.

There were bean bags, a small cloth bag of beans which you tried to throw through a hole in a piece of wood.

In 'Drat the Rat' there would be a 3 inch drainpipe stood up vertically. Someone would drop a home made rat-like creature in the top. You were supposed to hit the rat as it came out of the bottom of the pipe – it sounds easy, but it wasn't.

Then there was 'Find the Hidden Treasure', where you paid 6d for a small peg and put your name on it then stuck it in the ground which had been marked out in a 3ft square. A measurement had been recorded and sealed until the afternoon when the prizes were given out.

Darts, guess the weight of the cake or guess the name of the doll were other popular games.

Some of the younger children in fancy dress. See anyone you know?

An elegant group of ladies in period costume

A happy group taking tea

GARDEN FETE

AND

CLAY PIGEON SHOOT

WILL BE HELD IN

EMBSAY HOUSE GROUNDS

(BY KIND PERMISSION OF MR. AND MRS. J. IRESON)

ON

Saturday, 27th June, 1953

To be opened at 3

Mr. C. Brown (judge) and eager looking competitiors.

About to give the command to pull!

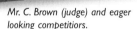

Pull!

A
GARDEN FETE

will be held at the

Embsay House Grounds
By kind permission of MR. and MRS. J. IRESON

SATURDAY, 23rd JULY 1955

Opened at 3 p.m. by
ALDERMAN & MRS. G. FLINTHAM, J.P.

BOWLING and SKITTLES for PIG
and many other Side-shows

BOYS INTER-SCHOOL FOOTBALL MATCH For Sh

Admission Sixpence.   Children Free

★

DANCE in Nocton Village H

Commencing 9 o'clock   Refreshments Aval

An attentive crowd at
a garden fete opening

Nocton R.A.F hospital
a popular venue for
garden fetes

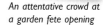

An outdoor game
creates some excite-
ment for young and
old alike

A bouquet for the
opener in appreciation
of her duties

A serious game demands serious attention

Children in fancy dress with their proud mothers looking on. Little Beau Peep clearly visible

Two ladies in summer frocks attending the home grown vegetable stall

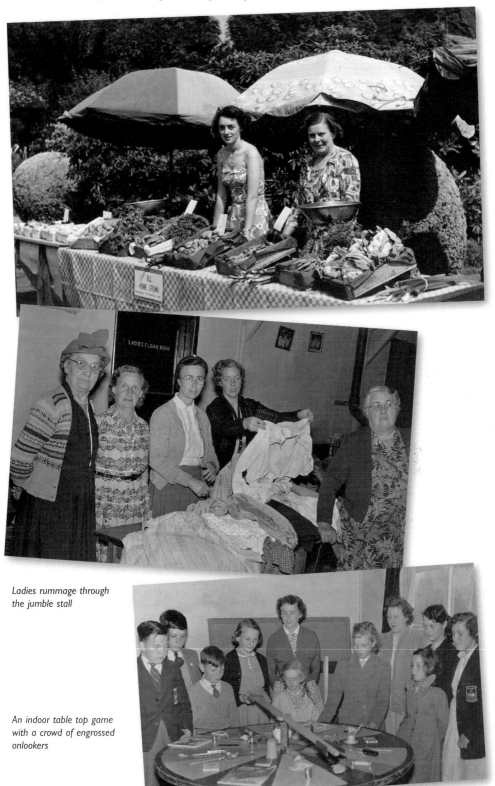

Ladies rummage through the jumble stall

An indoor table top game with a crowd of engrossed onlookers

The Lancaster bomber crash

In my first book I wrote about a Lancaster Bomber crashing in Potterhanworth Fen, in May 1943. I said this plane was from Bardney, but I have now been corrected by the pilot. In actual fact it came from Wickenby.

A 'friend of a friend' of mine went up north to a party, and an elderly gentleman came to talk to him. During the conversation my friend mentioned that he had come from Bardney, and the old chap said that the last time he was in Bardney was in 1945, when his Lancaster crashed. My friend was telling Mr Roger Audis, an aviation historian, about this meeting. Roger, also from Bardney, decided to arrange to meet the ex-pilot and interview him. This interview took place on the 10th September 2002 and was recorded on a cassette tape.

The pilot, Stan Howes, was flying the Wickenby Lancaster back to Wickenby from Germany the day before the crash and was almost there when an engine packed

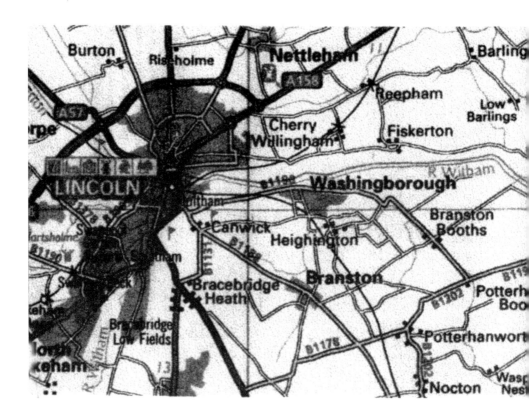

up, and he landed on three engines. He was informed that it would be repaired in time for him to fly the next day. The crew loaded up the next morning – they were Stan Howes (the pilot), Jack Cutliff (navigator), Bill Eastoe (bomb aimer), Frank Ford (wireless operator), Jim Warner (upper gunner) and Paddy Sheridon (tail gunner), Squadron 626.

As the Lancasters prepared to take off, the faulty engine caught fire, but as they were too near the end of the runway, they had to take off, and they were instructed to go to 1500 feet and bale out.

Billy Eastoe was caught in the top of a tree at Southery. When someone came to him, they told him to free the 'chute and jump down, to which Billy replied:

"You b....r off, I've got this far without an injury – I'm not going to break a leg jumping out of a tree! Fetch a ladder!"

The whole crew landed safely. When Stan, the last man out, was about to jump he noticed a parachute left by the door. He thought one of the crew had jumped without one, but it was too late to do anything about it. Thankfully, later he found out it was a spare.

The aircraft exploded in a potato field. A gang of men had just left the field, where they were hoeing potatoes, and had walked up the road to the farm, where they were in the barn having dinner. When they heard the crash and looked out, the 12 acre field was steaming all over...even now, 60 years later, parts of the aircraft are sometimes trailed to the end of the field by implements.

In Autumn 1986, when the tile drains were being put across the field, the trenching machine found the engine and propeller (pictured in my first book), which are now in the museum at East Kirkby.

The crew were flying again the next day on Manor trips over Holland, and later they carried soldiers back from Brussels.

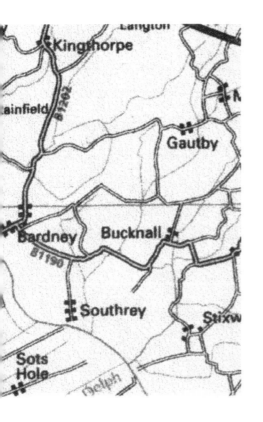

Wasp Nest Social Club and WI

The Wasp Nest Hall was used just like the other two Village Halls, although the members were spread throughout the fens. But the owners and directors of the Estate treated it like a small village, taking part in social functions such as fetes, dances and whist drives. In the 1950s there were regular dances held on Saturday nights in the Wasp Nest Hall. A bus would come from Bardney with the three man band in the back, and it would pick people up on its way through the fens. Many of these would be Irish seasonal workers who were staying in the farm buildings.

A report like this was sent to the Monthly Magazine about once a year:

"At our General Meeting held in the club in April 1950, we found that our finances were even better than the previous year. This was mainly due to the support of all the people that have helped us. On the 14th April a free social was held for members and guests; on this occasion the Cyril J Scott Darts Challenge Cup was played.

We also had the pleasure of the company of the Manger's wife, Mrs Ireson. During the evening she presented the cup to the winner, Mr A Sewell. Mr F Bark was runner up. Mrs Ireson also presented a replica to last year's winner, Mr J Worrall."

Author's note: This was the day when Mrs Ireson came in a large hat, something of which our older member had not seen the like before. One old member, Bill Gash, was reported to have said: 'Dunt she look a tw.. in that hat', which Mrs Ireson overheard and said 'Thank you, Bill!'

Back to the report:

"We have started off the third year in good style, and our two Whitsun dances were so well attended that we wondered where the people had come from, apart from the functions mentioned our members can be seen playing darts, dominoes, Honest John, Fling 'Em, etc. And the way some of them have been trained I feel sure some would beat some of those (Find the Lady) Gentlemen

Since the resignation of Rev. Healey, the Sunday School has been run by Mr & Mrs Redshaw, pending the induction of the new Vicar of Nocton. Meanwhile we are now preparing for our garden fete, which will be held in August."

Owing to the workers not having electric power in their cottages, and fresh water not being available in the fens, by the late 1950s workers had gradually moved up into the villages, for better, more up-to-date facilities. The Wasp Nest Hall was no longer needed, and the social club closed in 1959.

The social link with the RAF who had their hospital at Nocton Hall for many years is shown in this photograph. This was taken at Wasp Nest, Nocton Fen on the occasion of a visit by the RAF to a garden fete and garden party. Many social cricket and football matches and darts and domino nights were held in all three halls or gardens, those being Nocton, Dunston and WASP nest. 1956.

Some of the people present on the photograph are general managers wife Mrs. L. Ireson, M. Raisen, M. Johnson, Mrs Barks, Mrs Sands, G. Roberts, Mrs Johnson, Mrs. Chambers, Mrs. Wakefield, General Manager Mr. John Ireson sits in front with the children.

The annual outing to Skegness organised by the social club committee was on Sunday June 24th, when six coaches of children parents and friends made the trip. The children are each given 7s 6d pocket money. Coach ride free and half price tickets for their rides on the fun fair. All had a very happy day and arrived home safe but tired and well satisfied after a well organized outing.

A little Lincolnshire dialect

Ode Jorjie cum hoom from werk a bit unda th'wetha.

Hi went in th'owse, hi sed: 'Aja theer misis, wot du ya recen, I doont feel iva sa wel.'

'Noow, ja doont luk sa wel itha, ja luk awl yella, git off ta th'dokta.'

Soor off hi went ta th'dokta, an th'dokta sed 'Goor bak o' that screern an' tek ya cloors off.'

Wen hi cum owt th'dokta sed 'Ya arr reel yella, aren't ya? Thars a new complarnt gooin th'rowns an' I think yarve got it; it's so new that it ent bin given a narme. Weer calin it Yella 45, but that's th'gud noose; th'bad noose is yarve ony about a week t'live.'

'God, that's not much,' sai Jorje.

Soor hi nip home ta is misis an' teld her. She said, 'God, that's not much, if that's rate ya gewin ta git that muny out a th'poorst ofis an' weer gewin ta have a bludy gud time – ya cumin wi me ta bingo tanite.'

Hi sed 'Wot? I've niva bin ta bingo bifoor!'

'Well,' shi sed, 'Ya cumin tanite!'

Soor the got redy an' of tha went, got seten down an' got a tikit. Tha fella sed 'First garme is four cornas fo' undred powns.'

Abowt sevn numbas went an' Jorje showtid 'Ows' an' clected is muny.

Then th'blowk sed: 'Necst is avful hows fo'thowsan powns.'

Soor of the went ageen, an' the ent gon far wen ih showtid 'Ows'. The fela said: 'Cum up har an letz ring th'hed ofis, ja mitea got th'country flia, it's fifti thowsan powns.'

Soor mart rung up an'sed, 'Ya wun it, ya are a luki buga!'

'Luki buga?' sed Jorje, 'I've ony a week t'live, I've got Yella 45!'

'Well, buga me!' sed the showta, 'Jav wun th'rafel an awl!'

'Mornin, Jorje, I hev somat ta tel ya' sed Sam.

'Ow eja?'

'Yis I ev. Ya nor them new fangol moorta cars? Well, I wos ridin mi bike this mornin an' an ode hare cum runin' trate outa hedj bottom, just mist mi frunt weel. An' as he run cross tha roord a car wos cumin anit run ova it, an' theer it lar ded in the roord. Ded asa nit. I got off mi bike an' was stood theer lukin at the corpse an' th'fella in th'car went t'is boot and cum across th'roord to us, an hi ed one o'them aary sols. Hi jus gev th'hare acsquert an' it got up an run lie tha devil. I sed god, mart, that's bluddi gud stuff, wot isit? 'Or', hi sed, Ya can git it from tha chemist, its hartstora!'"

Laura Rasen and Claris Counsall picking potatoes.
Although this was hard back-breaking work, Laura could
raise a smile for the camera

Malc Reek baling barley straw with the Fordson Major
E27N and Massey-Harris 701 Baler

Cereal harvest on the Fen

Jack Smith, Tom Counsell and colleagues stooking wheat on Dunston Fen

Harvesting on Dunston Heath

Early Albion tipper lorry unloading into the dryer at Nocton, 1950's

A contractors crop sprayer in action. Note the futuristic looking cab on the Farmall tractor. This would give protection to the driver from any drift of dangerous chemical

Early mechanised harvesting on Nocton Heath. The two International Harvester self propelled combines heralded a new era in cereal harvesting

One of the first Massey 780's at work. Note the Smiths crisps logo on the grain tank

Harvesting on Dunston Heath

Combine driver, Les
Saunby and Lorry driver,
Bill Marshall unload the
combines grain tank

The fleet of 13 Massey Ferguson
combines taken from the roof af the
corn mill

780 Special's at work, Wasp Nest in the background

Eight combines cutting on Abbey Hill, just above Wasp Nest. Note the Poplar trees in the background, this is where the last owner of the estate's ashes are scattered. He wanted to be able to see right over his land, just like the lion king

Stacking bales from the 701 Baler. It would take a fit man to sledge behind one of today's high output machines

Peas and Sugar Beet

Herb Hodson making a grand job of ploughing with the 75hp Caterpillar tractor in 1950. The basis of a good crop of peas and sugar beet was a well ploughed field left to catch the winter frosts

Roy Sellors filling the 18ft Tullos artificial manure spreader with Fisons granulated fertilizer. Both peas and sugar beet required a lot of tillage

Bill Franklin and Harold Freeston swathing peas with
Hume pea cutters. It must have taken a little while to
get used to driving in reverse

Weeding sugar beet, a labour intensive operation

An early mechanised sugar beet harvester meant lifting
was much easier than by hand, although the four wheel
rulley would have to be unloaded by men with beet forks

Bob Kettleborough with the Catchpole Cadet. The Ferguson tipping trailer would make life much easier, although a horse and cart can just be seen on the headland

L. Massam cleans soil from the Standen Solobeet using a Massey-Ferguson 35 power unit. Note good provision of lights for working after dark

Potatoes: what the estate was famous for

Maurice Hall with the John Deere and potato spinner

Dan Wilford hoovering out pototoes on Nocton Fen

Dan Wilford on Fordson Diesel Major with elevator potato digger

A gang of ladies rapidly fill the basket after the hoover has passed. The children lend a hand

Dec Sellors and George Bond emptying baskets into the Fergi trailer on Dunston Fen

Ron Brazier and Fred Norrell put the finishing touches to a quarter of a mile long potato clamp

Riddling potatoes on the fen. The young lad looks very business like in his overalls

Tommy Flintham, George Baxter and Percy Ward riddling
potatoes from one of the many clamps. Todays safety
inspector would have had a field day!

Al Bee, Percy Bell, Ron Duckering loading the old lorry
with sacks of potatoes after riddling. Note the weigh and
weights but no winding up barrow!

Is that a "hicking stick" in his hand. This probably explains the lack of a winding up barrow

Loading potatoes onto the farm's railtruck's after riddling

A more civilized method of loading with the Cook elevator

Sid Smith and Al Bee pose for the photographer outside the workshops at Nocton before leaving for the factory at Lincoln

The Smith's Potato Crisp factory, Newark Road, Lincoln,
once a major employer of the city

Sid Smith looking justifiably proud of his load after
arriving at the crisp factory in Lincoln

Loading one of the delivery vans in the factory

Fortunately a box of crisps weighed very little, as the delivery lorries carried a row of boxes on the top deck, the only means of getting them up there was by hand

A delivery lorry sets out to help "Feed the Nation" as described on the lorries livery. Note the row of boxes on the top deck with sheet rolled up over the cab

The new bulk potato store. Wasp Nest, Nocotn Fen

Snippets from the news

Rustlers in Lincolnshire 1951

As reported in the Daily Telegraph.

Police in South Lincolnshire are searching for sheep rustlers who carried out a night time raid at Nocton, near Lincoln; the biggest black market job for years.

They escaped with 40 breeding lambs and ewes worth about £400, taken from Smith's Potato Estate. All the sheep were marked with a red dot and branded with 'PE'.

The thieves must have had a double decked lorry, which was driven along a very isolated farm road between Potter-hanworth and Nocton. Gates were taken off their hinges and used as pens. Tyre marks left by the lorry were examined by the CID.

The theft was discovered by the general manager, Mr John Ireson, on Wednesday morning.

Working shepherd, David Rumbelow with his dog Bonnie on the Nocton Farms estate

Lived by catching moles: and in fifty years he trapped over 300,000!

From The Standard, (circa 1960)

How many people earn their living by catching moles? Not many today, but that is how Mr Jeremiah Sutton, of Front Street, Dunston, lived for nearly 50 years, until he was almost 81. And one year Mr Sutton counted the moles he caught. The total? Over 6,000!

"And that was only an ordinary year," Mr Sutton told a 'Standard' reporter.

So in his 50 years of mole catching it is estimated that Mr Sutton cleared the land, from a wide area surrounding Dunston, of over 300,000 moles. And of course, as well as being paid for catching them, he was able to sell the mole-skins, all of which he sent to Cambridge.

It was in 1896 that Mr Sutton moved to Nocton, going into service with Mr John Hudson at Nocton Hall, for whom he became a waggoner. Ten years later he moved to Dunston.

Crossbred ewes and lambs on Dunston Heath March 1950

Fattening sheep on Swedes, Dunston heath 1950

A century of change

Jim Harvey and Bill Scratcheard in the slaughter house with pig carcases, 1950, long before the days of hygiene inspectors

Six Masssey-Harris 780 combines at work in one field. To see six combines together today would be a rare sight

I often sit and think awhile about the changes we have seen
There will never be so many again, what a lot there's been!

Down on the farms in Lincolnshire when I was just a lad
Steam engines and horses were going, it was really sad.

New tractors and lorries, and mechanical machines
Were being introduced to farming - what a changing scene.

More and more motorcars were coming out on the road
The trains were being withdrawn to give the lorries their load.

The Lancaster bomber – four engines with props spinning-
Were up against the new jet engine, and the latter were winning.

The oil lamps were going and new electric ones brighter
The spitfire was going, replaced by a jet fighter.

The changes were coming quicker than ever,
Labouring jobs disappearing – you had to be clever.

The old wringer, or mangle, was replaced by the spin dryer
Gas and electricity replace the coal fire.

What a great change there's been on the telephone lines
And computers send messages round the world in next to no time.

Men have looked down on the earth from the moon
Some life form will be found on a planet very soon.

Where the old radio stood in the corner of your home
A television now brings pictures of the millennium dome.

Now you can have breakfast in London, and lunch in New York
Or you can commute to Paris from London to work.

Millions of cars have replaced bicycles and trams
And you don't see many babies being pushed out in prams.

The microwave oven, another machine to help the housewife,
Hundreds and thousands of changes during my life.

World War 2 we struggled through, with many lives lost.
Now we're giving our country away, was it worth the cost?

There will be many more inventions during the next hundred years
But surely not as many changes as we have seen here.

Len Woodhead

A miscellany of memories

Author, Len Woodhead - Farm Foreman presents Mrs. I. Baxter with her retirement gift which was given by her old friends and work colleagues on the Nocton estate. Her husband George looks on

Rod Hargreaves presents author Len Woodhead and Ken Williamson with a gift from previous workmates after leaving the estate. Their proud wives look on

Nocton church bell ringers all of whom were estate employees, having a total of 197 years work between them

Nocton and Dunston Youth Club sponsored walk

Dunston village hall beauty queen contest 1950 - 1951. It must have been difficult to pick the winner

Mrs. Bill Redshaw retires as president of Nocton WI

Sailors, Anne Noble, Janet Saunby and Joan Day as HMS Nocton at the estates football club fete 1954

144 children attended the Christmas party in 1959.
They received crisps from directors and crackers from
Mr and Mrs E. M. Howard. The estate employees
children received a handkerchief each from the directors

Presentation of cups at Dunston sports club dinner. Mr.
Frank Smith on the far right, his wife second on the left

Staff dinner 5th January 1954. Where you there?

POTATO   **SMITHS**   **ESTATES**
LIMITED

SECOND

Staff Dinner

Held at

LINCOLN

TUESDAY, 5TH JANUARY

1954

Chairman
MR. JOHN IRESON

An innocent looking Len Woodhead, the author, sits on the right

Nocton Village Hall opened 28th September 1946

Nocton Village Hall receives a Spring clean 1975

Embassy garden fete 27th June 1953. The trophies on the table are for the winners of the clay pigeon shoot. The head keeper stands in trilby hat

Ploughing match luncheon 1950

*General view of cottages, railway junctions and farm
buildings showing typical fen district, Wasp Nest 1950's*

*Modern cottages and a well maintained dredged dyke,
Wasps Nest 1950*

A Lincolnshire lad looks ahead

The Future of English Farming as I see it.

Small farms will disappear within the next five years – anything under 500 acres will not be profitable enough to carry on. Old family farms will go, swallowed up by large financial groups, and a lot of contract farming will be the thing. Encouraged by the Government and the brains of the EEC, the small farms are being strangled off their land.

Farmers markets are being formed, but they are only a very small part of the help farming needs today. Even if they do get going they will never compete with the large supermarkets – if they looked like doing so the supermarkets would price them out of the market, just as they have done to our dairy farms. We needn't look at our schools for low marks – our Government is in the same league.

You just have to look at our representatives in the EEC over the last ten or fifteen years; anyone who has been unable to make the grade at home has been allocated a lovely comfortable post in Brussels. Can you think of anything that we can say has been in our favour? Fishing? Weights and Measures? Anything – crop or animal products – that has benefited our countryside? Look at the setaside. What a mess. How many trees are coming down to make the paper that our farmers are having to read - forms to fill in - their job used to be producing, not sitting in an office looking and listening for the next episode coming from Brussels. Some of the finest land in the world is being dumped into setaside. We could produce enough food for the starving in Africa twice over. Instead of sending money for some high-up statesmen in these countries to launder somewhere else in a hidden bank account, we could send food.

And look at the energy crisis – coal mines have been closed, no-one wants a nuclear power station, no-one wants a wind turbine, but they want the luxuries of electricity. Look at the oil, what a lot of problems it creates, with Iraq and Iran, and many more that we don't even hear about. While we sit still as we are doing on looking for a replacement for oil, the Government can just keep grabbing the tax.

The smoker is being pushed out so the Government will loose a lot of tax, and they are going to overcome that by opening the pubs for longer – more pints, more tax.

Sugar beet will disappear from our farms within the next five years; it will all be grown in the Eastern Block. But we have good land, instead of producing nothing we could have biodegradable energy from a rapeseed oil crop, and also sugar – it's on the doorstep, why are we waiting? I will tell you it would cost to produce it – not like oil, once its found turn the taps on and off as required and in rolls the tax – there wouldn't be much scope for revenue from beet and rape, but what there would be is a countryside looked after like it was in the past, not vast areas grown knee high with rubbish like nettles and thistles that no-one can walk through. Most of all it would give the countryman his pride back by giving him the living he is happy with and making us proud of our country once again. The only problem is, have we still got a country, or has it been signed or given away? If so, let's be getting it back – we can govern ourselves better than the Brussels mob.